PowerKiDS Readers
Happy Holidays!

I0803802

Halloween

Josie Keogh

PowerKiDS press
New York

For Heath

Published in 2013 by The Rosen Publishing Group, Inc.
29 East 21st Street, New York, NY 10010

First Edition

Editor: Amelie von Zumbusch
Book Design: Andrew Povolny

Photo Credits: Cover Digital Vision/Getty Images; p. 5 Stockbyte/Thinkstock; p. 7 Comstock Images/Getty Images; p. 9 KidStock/Blend Images/Getty Images; p. 11 Pixland/Thinkstock; p. 13 Ariel Skelley/The Images Bank/Getty Images; p. 15 Jupiterimages/Workbook Stock/Getty Images; p. 17 Franz Marc Frei/LOOK/Getty Images; p. 19 Jupiterimages/Comstock/Thinkstock; pp. 21, 23 iStockphoto/Thinkstock.

Library of Congress Cataloging-in-Publication Data

Keogh, Josie.
Halloween / by Josie Keogh. — 1st ed.
p. cm. — (Powerkids readers: happy holidays!)
Includes index.
ISBN 978-1-4488-9623-3 (library binding) — ISBN 978-1-4488-9702-5 (pbk.) —
ISBN 978-1-4488-9703-2 (6-pack)
1. Halloween—Juvenile literature. I. Title.
GT4965.K45 2013
394.2646–dc23

2012020044

Manufactured in the United States of America

CPSIA Compliance Information: Batch #W13PK3: For Further Information contact Rosen Publishing, New York, New York at 1-800-237-9932

Contents

Halloween is fun!

It began as a feast called Samhain.

Kids trick-or-treat.

They get candy!

They dress up.

A **princess** is the top costume for kids.

New York has the biggest **parade**.

You can carve a **pumpkin**.

Pumpkins grow on vines.

Illinois grows the most pumpkins.

WORDS TO KNOW

parade

princess

pumpkins

INDEX

WEBSITES

Due to the changing nature of Internet links, PowerKids Press has developed an online list of websites related to the subject of this book. This site is updated regularly. Please use this link to access the list:
www.powerkidslinks.com/pkrhh/hallo/